A LEGENDARY LINE:

Silverton to Durango

A Photo Album

Published by Magnum Offset Printing Inc
Design by SJS Design (Susan Smilanic)

ISBN: 1-890437-40-9
Second Edition

TABLE OF CONTENTS

Courtesy: Duane A. Smith

THE AGE OF THE RAILROAD

Speaking of railroads, Mark Twain observed that one he rode on did not quite measure up to expectations. "It was one of those trains that gets tired every seven minutes and stops to rest three quarters of an hour.... Next year we will walk." Bedeviled by a slow or tardy train, generations of Americans might have felt likewise.

Those generations of Americans who grew up with the railroad as their major means, or at least an important means, of transportation never forgot the experience. The thundering engine, the lonesome whistle at night, the excitement of a meal in a dining car or the night in a Pullman berth, the fun of counting cars as they raced by the crossing, the thrill of waiting at the station to go somewhere new, the romance of steam trains—they all left a lasting impression on one's memory.

Most nineteenth-century Americans, despite such inconveniences as Twain complained of, fell in love with the railroad, almost from the time it first chugged and smoked onto the American scene. The country was young and burdened by the twin problems of distance and isolation, problems greater than their European forebears had ever faced. The railroad seemed the logical answer because it could go almost anywhere, run year-round in all weather, was faster, and eventually became safer and more comfortable than whatever else was available. Was there anything more luxurious than the Pullman car in its heyday, or the railroad owner's private car? To add to its blessings, the railroad usually carried freight and passengers more cheaply than any of its transportation competitors.

Other nations have railroad history, yet none of these countries have been so shaped by railroads as the United States. Because of our vast continental spaces and virgin lands beyond the Mississippi River, railroads played a major role in our history. As the country grew, they tied east to west, but failed to tie north to south, and helped bring on the great American tragedy, the Civil War. They helped the north to win the war, a war that prepared men, equipment, and leadership for the great post-war railroad boom. Railroads, in fact, touched upon all aspects of American life in the nineteenth century. They helped shape the destiny of eastern seaport cities such as New York and were a major factor in the emergence of Chicago. Railroads sired communities throughout the United States. A town or village without a railroad connection was poor indeed, a victim of community "bad breath." There are ghost towns, or bypassed stunted villages, throughout the country that mark their forward march. Railroads were there to help the rise of big business, of which they emerged as its most outward and common symbols. In fact, railroads were the nation's first big business. They brought together the iron ore, coal, workers, and markets to make Pittsburgh the iron and steel heart of America. The "iron horse" carried immigrants, tourists, and manufactured goods out west and brought western products back east. Railroads promoted, developed, dominated, and, if needed, destroyed. They developed natural resources such as coal, timber, and land, transporting people to them and shipping their products (coal, timber, and crops) to market. They became almost indispensable to American growth and development. Before the century ended, Americans both loved and hated, needed and despised, railroads. No matter, hardly anything seemed more significant to Americans of that day. American ingenuity rose to the occasion, and our railroads became the cutting edge for new ideas, technology, and inventions that revolutionized railroading throughout the world. More powerful engines, specialized freight cars, the Pullman car, better braking systems, the telegraph to regulate schedules, new road building techniques—American railroads had them all and more, even some shady corporation and political shenanigans. Throw in a good dash of corruption, and graft came in its wake.

The railroad brought change to hamlet and town, to farm and mine, to ranch and store, to factory and city, to state capital and town council, and to mountain, prairie, seaport, and tourist meccas. That change undergirded the birth of modern America, that change became modern America.

As a people, we came to romanticize those trains as they rumbled across the continent, spreading hope to everyone, unless one happened to be in their way. They symbolized the strength of this new nation. Young America, we often called ourselves. We romanticized railroads, too, in song, verse, and illustration. The melody and words of "The Wabash Cannon Ball" ring down the decades to touch Americans' memories and minds.

From the calm Pacific waters,

To the rough Atlantic shore,

Ever climbing hills and mountains,

Like no other did before.

She's as graceful as a comet,

Smoother than a water fall,

It's the Western combination,

It's the Wabash Cannon Ball.

("Wabash Cannon Ball," 1940)

That mythical train to everywhere has never stopped running!

It is all gone now, my friends. Railroad track mileage reached its peak in Colorado in the 1890s, and in the United States in 1916, just before the country entered World War I. After that, mileage has steadily declined. Only in a few places can that era of steam, smoke, and steel be relived. You are about to read a story of one of those surviving lines, the Durango to Silverton.

Eternal mystery of the railroad. Why is he stopping the train?

FROM BIRTH TO BOOM

Americans may have fallen in love with railroads, and we, as a result, emerged as their leading nineteenth-century proponents. Nevertheless, we did not create the idea or develop the first railroad lines. Our English cousins did that. Around the time of our second war for "independence" with them, the War of 1812, a steam engine began the regular hauling of coal wagons over a track. Completion of the first true railroad followed in 1825. In September, an engine hauled its tender, twelve cars of coal and flour, a box-like passenger coach filled with directors, and twenty-one open freight "wagons," fitted with temporary seats, for the common folk. The track's gauge, the distance between the inner edges of the two rails, was four feet, eight and one-half inches. By 1829, a locomotive traveled thirty-five miles per hour. The railroad era had been born.

Did the United States need the railroad at this time? When it took fifty days to move freight from New York to Cincinnati, and thirty-nine hours by "fast stage" to go from New York to Boston, one would suspect the country had a crying need. The exciting news of what was happening in England reached the former colonies, and curious American engineers visited the island to see what was happening.

The interest soon surfaced for an American railroad. Unfortunately, the United States had entered a canal craze, thanks to the grand success of New York's Erie Canal. Interest marched upward, but financial support did not duplicate it. Nor did stagecoach operators, canal folks, turnpike owners, and other vested businesses think highly of this new idea. Northern men were very enthused, but southerners succeeded in getting the first trains running.

The merchants of Charleston, South Carolina, needed to improve their inland trade from the rich cotton-growing back country. They succeeded. On Christmas Day, 1830, the first scheduled steam railroad train carried 141 passengers. By 1833, the line ran 136 miles. But, the South soon dropped behind. With an excellent system of rivers, and with the ease of access for steamboats to carry the bulk cotton more economically than railroads, southern leaders failed to keep up their momentum.

Meanwhile, the Baltimore and Ohio, despite an 1828 charter, stayed on hold, until 1831, with horse-drawn cars. Then, in the summer of 1831, a steam engine proved its worth, although not until 1852 did the railroad reach the Ohio River. Boston, New York City, and Philadelphia soon joined the fray to control trade and traffic. A railroad craze swiftly affected the North and Midwest.

Nothing unusual about that. Americans suffered through numerous crazes—gold, silver, copper, land, for example—before the century waned.

By 1840, approximately 3,000 miles of track had been laid, far outstripping England and Europe, which fell short of 2,000 miles of rail. That was only the prelude to the great railroad building era. American railroads were mostly located in the Atlantic states, from New Hampshire to South Carolina. It was a thin, disjointed system; however, the future appeared to be fascinating.

And that is what it proved to be. Twenty years later America had more than 30,000 miles of track, with more than a billion dollars invested in the industry. Railroads had become the transportation miracle of the present, not a dream for the future. Earlier, in 1856, a railroad bridge spanned the Mississippi River over the objections of rival steamboat interests. Railroads moved westward beyond the river, and already people talked of a transcontinental route. The race to the West had begun. Indeed, a railroad was already out there in the West. The same year the bridge across the Mississippi was completed, California's first railroad started operation. The West had embarked by moving eastward. No longer would the frontier be a simple westward movement.

Despite their earlier start, the Atlantic seaboard states fell behind the Midwest. Ohio and Illinois ranked first and second in rail mileage in 1860, with Indiana coming in a strong fifth. Chicago, serviced by eleven different railroads that year, had become America's leading railroad center. Gaining that status had come about amazingly quickly; it had not been until 1848 that the first line opened from the city. Eight years later, its chief railroad, the Illinois Central, finished its initial main line of seven hundred miles of track, the longest railroad in the world.

Americans' pride knew no bounds, and without question, the country had forged way ahead of the rest of the world in railroading. However, firsts and statistics do not begin to tell the whole story. Railroading was being born. From humble beginnings, it had reached the threshold of maturity in a generation.

Americans loved the speed and the ease of rail transportation. By 1852, for example, rail shipments from Cincinnati to New York City took from six to eight days. Compared to the time of wagon transportation, this was revolutionary The trip from Baltimore to Wheeling, West Virginia, lasted several days by stagecoach, sixteen hours by train. Railroad freight rates, while higher than canal rates, still gave the shipper unanswered advantages over wagons, canal boats, and stages. The less efficient and poorly located canals disappeared first, and eventually they were all gone. Teamsters with their wagons became feeders for the railroads as did stages, with their passengers and mail. In the 1850s, Americans had solved the problem of moving people and goods both cheaply and quickly over the growing distances of their nation. The railroad had achieved a position of dominance that it would retain throughout the rest of the nineteenth century.

The democratic American passenger car. English actress Fanny Kemble was not impressed

A host of inventions and new ideas speeded the railroads along. It took experimentation in those early years, but Americans proved up to the challenge. The *American Railroad Journal* first appeared in 1831 and was soon filled with technical and engineering articles. One of the earliest issues discussed sources of power to pull the trains. Steam power won out, just like in England, but not until horses pulling (or even walking on treadmills as motive power!), and sails and wind had been discarded as impractical.

It took about twenty years for the railroads to settle on a basic design for their steam locomotives. This design became known as the "American" type, a "4-4-0." The set of numbers described the wheel arrangement on the locomotive. The first figure gives the wheels on the leading truck. The second lists the driving wheels and the last number, here zero, the number of wheels on the trailing axle.

This type of locomotive proved excellent for the needs of the day, light in weight, flexible, and powerful enough to handle most of the work required of it.

They had simply laid the first tracks on the ground, a practical, though an unsuitable, arrangement. Devising a roadbed was a step in the right direction. Then came the decision for material for the tracks. Wood proved too short lived, so long iron straps were fastened to wood. The iron straps had a tendency to work loose and curl during use, creating "snakeheads." These, quite often, sprang up, breaking through the floor of passing cars. With passenger cars, that could be a chilling and deadly experience. The answer was the iron rail, and the most practical shape the T-rail, although on some branch lines the strap-iron rails stayed in use until the Civil War.

What to place the rails on created another quandry. Simply placing them on a roadbed was not the answer. Thawing and freezing, not to mention the problems of rain soaked earth, made that plan unsatisfactory. Fastening the rails to blocks of granite, or other stone, was tried initially yet failed to provide an adequate answer and gave a hard ride to both cars and passengers. The most satisfactory answer came to be wood crossties imbedded in a gravel roadbed. That resolved two issues—the use of the best material and always keeping an accurate, equal distance between the two rails. Spiked down rails ended concerns about proper distance to maintain the gauge.

What gauge to build presented another question. Those early railroads, purchasing English locomotives, used four feet, eight and a half inches (standard gauge) out of necessity. Variations soon appeared, however. Sometimes, because of an owner's whim, geographic conditions, or to prevent the loss of traffic to a rival, another size was chosen. By the time of the Civil War, gauges ranged from three feet to six feet. This hurt railroading, in general, but it was particularly bad among the few southern lines in existence. As the war neared, however, the standard gauge became the most accepted. Not until the 1890s would uniformity finally appear, with only a few narrow gauge (three feet) routes holding out.

As the railroad chugged through a pasture repeated collisions with prize cattle (and not so prize cattle, who thereupon often became "prize") and other farm animals made the appearance of the cowcatcher a necessity. This still left undecided the responsibility and the damage payment. For decades, this proved to be a contentious issue for the railroads to handle, even after they took the second logical step, fencing in the right-of-way. The steam-whistle arrived in the mid-thirties. It was used to signal the train crews and also to warn pedestrians, alert everybody at crossings, and, hopefully, encourage animals to remove themselves from the tracks.

Night travel presented another problem. Until the 1840s, very few trains ran at night. Pushing a small flatcar with a fire burning on it was not the best solution. The answer came with the headlight, using kerosene and tin reflectors. Placed on the front of the locomotive, it helped, along with the cowcatcher, to create the familiar profile, once the cab was enclosed to give the engineer and fireman more protection. In the colder New England and Midwestern winters, it kept them from freezing.

Winter weather caused another predicament—slippery and frozen tracks threatening to cause accidents or even to bring train movements to a halt. Actually, though, a plague of grasshoppers in Pennsylvania in 1836 brought the sandbox into operation to increase wheel traction. A more important improvement came with the invention of the swivel wheel, which was mounted on the truck under the front of the locomotive. That allowed trains to negotiate curves easily and at a faster speed.

One of the problems, as mileage grew and trains increased, was how to keep them all on schedule and on the tracks without collisions or time-consuming delays. There had been some appalling accidents. The answer was at hand. Samuel Morse conceived the electromagnetic telegraph, and it answered the obvious need, to send messages rapidly over long distances. After the first telegraph line was laid in 1844, its significance soon became obvious.

It did not take the railroads long to realize the significance of this invention to their business. The Erie Railroad took advantage of a parallel telegraph line, and in September 1851, started using the telegraph to dispatch trains. It worked so well that all the railroads would soon adopt the practice. The settled portions of the country, by the early 1850s, were well supplied with telegraphic communications.

The evolution of the cars pulled by the locomotives proved fascinating. Passenger cars, at first, looked like a stagecoach set on wheels, running down a track. It was not long, however, before the more familiar corridor down the middle of the passenger cars emerged (in the early 1830s). The English actress, Fanny Kemble, left this description of a car she rode in during an American tour. The car, she felt, looked "like a long greenhouse upon wheels; the seat which each contain[s] two persons (a pretty tight fit, too), are placed down the whole length of the vehicle." Fanny was not impressed with the democracy of the aisle, as opposed to the British "compartment" system. The aisle seemed "for the uneasy to fidget up and down, for the tobacco-chewers to spit in, and for a whole tribe of itinerant fruit and cake-sellers to rush through."

Fanny was not the only one who complained, because despite the speed and convenience, riding in a pre-Civil War train could be uncomfortable and downright stressful. The stiff-back seats proved uncomfortable, and tight, too, as Fanny complained, if two well-endowed adults sat down. The stove (or stoves) near the ends of the car roasted those near them, while the folks in the middle froze. The cars jerked when the train stopped and started; modern automatic couplings remained decades in the future. Vendors, passing up and down the cars, peddling everything from hot bricks for

one's feet to something to eat, could be annoying, rude, and aggressive. On a bad day, a passenger could get all three, with one person hawking his or her wares.

As the need arose, familiar cars appeared on the scene. Locomotives soon pulled flatcars, boxcars, coal cars, and others. The small size of the cars kept the volume down, but even more troublesome was the manual braking, one car at a time, and the coupling of the cars. This made railroading both dangerous and slow. The slowness in individually braking each car also led to some serious accidents, as they could not stop trains in time.

By the time of the Civil War, American railroads had come a long way. Notwithstanding that, railroads definitely needed yet to travel farther for safety, convenience, improved freight capacity, and a host of other matters. Even such a small thing as "time" threw them off schedule and cost money and inconveniences. Towns and individuals ran on God's time, New York time, sun time, Chicago time—whatever they wished in this era of rugged individualism with one's watch.

There were no standard time zones. Imagine trying to create a schedule and operate a railroad under such conditions. One newspaper story commented that Illinois had twenty-seven and neighboring Wisconsin thirty-eight different local times. Another study showed that, while it was noon in Washington, D.C., Boston clocks had reached 12:24 and Richmond's 12:31. Endless confusion reigned. Travelers complained, but to no avail at the moment.

Similar, if less pressing, confusion could be seen in various reactions to the coming of the iron horse. Poet Emily Dickinson liked them. Almost a recluse living in Amherst, Massachusetts, she felt that the railroad virtually intruded into her life. In "Punctual as a Star," she described the locomotive as "docile and omnipotent."

> I like to see it lap the miles,
> And lick the valleys up.
> And stop to feed itself at tanks:
> And then, prodigious, step.

The "Fresh Mail" Railroad prints were popular in parlors of homes.

Yet its "horrid, hooting stanza" broke the silence and interrupted her meditation. Henry Thoreau watched the trains go past Walden Pond with equally mixed emotions. When the locomotive rolled by, he wrote in **Walden**, "I hear the iron horse make the hills echo with his snort like thunder, shaking the earth with his feet, and breathing fire and smoke from his nostrils..., it seems as if the earth had got a race now worthy to inhabit it." One thing he felt was happening, the railroad was transforming America. "The startings and arrivals of the cars are now the epochs in the village day. Have not men improved somewhat in punctuality since the railroad was invented? To do things 'railroad fashion' is now the byword," Thoreau complained

At the same time, Thoreau bemoaned the disappearance of the old quiet rural ways and the appearance of noise, "the whistle of the locomotive penetrates my woods summer and winter...informing me that many restless city merchants are arriving... I will not have my eyes put out and ears spoiled by its smoke and steam and hissing." He saw jobs being lost and the "pastoral life whirled past and away." His neighbor and friend, Ralph Waldo Emerson, disagreed, "Railroad iron is a magician's rod in its power to evoke the sleeping energies of land and water." Another neighbor left no doubt about his feelings. Nathaniel Hawthorne described the locomotive as looking "much more like a sort of mechanical demon, that would hurry us to the infernal regions, than a laudable contrivance for smoothing our way to the Celestial City." No one could have been more emphatic than an Ohio school board, when it declared steam railroads "a device of the State to lead the immortal soul down to hell." Several states with huge canal investments actually passed restrictive laws against the iron horse.

The railroad was hardly out of its teenage years when the debate was launched. Did it positively or negatively influence and transform Americans and America? The rest of the nineteenth century would be increasingly caught up in that debate, until it spread from literary circles to main street saloons, and from the halls of Congress to church pulpits.

While some folks might debate the importance and impact of the railroad on Americans and America, there could be no question about the increasing role of the iron horse on the American scene.

As early as the 1830s, a few Americans dreamed of a transcontinental railroad. That was too early, from the technical aspect, but more importantly the United States did not even own much of the territory over which the rails would have to pass. Popular interest in the idea grew in the 1840s and, with the conclusion of the Mexican War in 1848, control of the land needed to be switched to the United States.

Meanwhile, various Midwestern and southern cities fancied themselves becoming the eastern terminus of such a proposed route. Chicago raced to a head start, but Milwaukee, St. Louis,

Memphis, Vicksburg, and New Orleans were not ready to let such a prospect slip away. Three potential routes were being discussed; a northern route through today's Minnesota to the west coast, a central route from the Missouri River via the South Pass region to the coast, and a southern route via Texas and westward. Of the three, the northern and middle routes went through much unsettled territory, as did the southern route beyond eastern Texas. The best weather route, but the longest, went south. Railroads prior to this time had been built through settled territory with built-in trade and passenger traffic, though not so in the West.

Technical problems of building such a railroad had been solved by the decade of the fifties. The dilemma now became mostly one of finance. It generally seemed agreed that any railroad across the continent would prove so speculative that construction entirely by private interests would be highly unlikely. Construction by the government flew contrary to the prevailing sentiment, that business activities were best run by individuals. The financial debate centered on the amount and type of government assistance that would be needed.

At this point, as the country entered the 1850s, the growing sectionalism joined the fray. One of the first results of this came with the Gadsden Purchase in 1853 from Mexico. To help southerners strengthen their bid for the transcontinental railroad, their Congressmen had pushed for the acquisition of this land of Apaches, saguaro cactus, and sand, in what is now southern Arizona. Onto the railroad stage came Illinois Senator Stephen Douglas, spokesman of Chicago interests. To make the central route more attractive and speed America's manifest destiny of settling the West, he introduced his Kansas-Nebraska bill to create these two territories. Settlement and the railroad would advance hand in hand. To get southern backing, Douglas advanced the idea of "popular sovereignty," or the right of the settlers to vote slavery in or out. Stunned northerners were appalled, and abolitionists infuriated, by Douglas's action. The Compromise of 1820 prohibited slavery in that region. The riotous debate that followed, before eventual passage, was surpassed by what was described as "Bleeding Kansas." That miniature civil war took railroad planning off the front page. Then the economic panic of 1857 and subsequent depression captured the public's attention. Finally, in October 1859, John Brown's raid at Harper's Ferry brought the country on the threshold of war.

With the election of Abraham Lincoln in 1860, and the firing on Fort Sumter in Charleston harbor the next April, the country plunged into Civil War. In the four war years that followed, the railroad came of age as a military weapon and component for victory. The American Civil War became the first railroad war. The north profited, while the south's lack of railroads helped lead to its defeat. And what lines the Confederacy had were overburdened to near halt or were the victims of wartime destruction.

All northern railroads benefited from increased wartime traffic; some for the first time paid dividends to stockholders. Unlike their southern counterparts, they were beyond the war zone, except for the Baltimore and Ohio. Northerners even found time to add another 4,000 miles to the northern system.

Equally as important for the future of railroads were the management and operational skills being acquired by northern railroad men. Never before had the lines been so pressured to handle large shipments of goods and heavy passenger loads. As the northern armies advanced, construction crews learned the art of building and repairing tracks and bridges-and redoing them again after a Confederate cavalry raid. Particularly fascinating, bridges were built in record time to carry heavy loads, even though President Lincoln thought they seemed to be constructed of nothing but "beanpoles and cornstalks."

By the end of the war, American railroads were strengthened and more efficient than they had ever been. Skilled management people, engineers, and track laying and bridge building crews stood ready for the post-war years. New methods of running and operating railroads had been found, and the conversion from iron to steel rails and from wood to coal was well started. Railroads had proven their worth in wartime, and now they leaped into peacetime with a new vigor. The golden age of railroads was at hand.

One other thing had happened during the war that shaped the railroad's future. The withdrawal of the south gave northerners a free hand at planning for the transcontinental railroad. The central route was chosen, and on July 1, 1862, President Lincoln signed the first Pacific Railway Bill. A second bill followed two years later. The Union Pacific Railroad was designated to build westward from Council Bluffs, Iowa (although Omaha became the real terminus), and the Central Pacific Railroad was to build eastward from Sacramento.

To overcome some of the financial problems, Uncle Sam presented each a two-hundred-foot right-of-way and ten alternate sections of government domain on each side of the right-of-way for every mile of track laid. A government subsidy of $16,000 per mile of road constructed over the prairie, and $32,000 per mile through the Rocky and Sierra Nevada Mountains, helped immeasurably. The companies also were given the right to use building materials from the public domain. The bargain had been struck between private enterprise and the federal government. Let the building begin.

The Central Pacific broke ground in January 1863 and, once across the valley, promptly ran into mountain construction. Building started in December 1863 on the Union Pacific. Wartime problems and difficulty in finding investors slowed advancement to a crawl. By the end of the war, the tracks reached only forty miles beyond Omaha. That in no way dampened the enthusiasm of supporters. Optimism soared. One, carried away in a flight of feverish fervor, expounded, "It was said of the Nile that it was a god. I think the Pacific Railroad project comes nearer being the subject of deification than anything else I have ever heard in the Senate. Everyone is trying to show his zeal in worshiping the road."

Congress only reflected the attitudes of many victorious northerners and over-joyed westerners. They could not wait to get that railroad built. Out there beyond the sunrise or sunset, depending on what company one worked for, lay untapped natural resources. Both Colorado and Nevada proved that. Farm land for union veterans, and others, just begged to be homesteaded; that was another Republican promise that had been fulfilled along with the railroad. Not only that, but land, business opportunities, town building, and a host of other profit making ideas were a heart beat away. The West was about to be opened, settled, and exploited.

Courtesy: National Archives

Railroads helped the North win the Civil War.

Courtesy: National Archives

Moving the "Monitor" during the seige of Petersburg.

A LIVELY TIME

As the railroads rushed from the west and from the east to join somewhere along the way, Americans stopped to consider the implications of the late war and the iron horse's spread of manifest destiny throughout the West. At long last, the east and west would be tied together, and what this meant excited their imaginations. North and south had split apart and were forcibly brought back together. Northerners now looked for new fields to conquer.

Mark Twain, who had just finished his newspaper reporter days at the Comstock's Virginia City, observed, "How solemn and beautiful is the thought that the earliest pioneer of civilization, the van-leader of civilization, is never the steamboat, never the railroad, never the newspaper, never the Sabbath-school teacher, never the missionary—but always whisky!" Cynical, but truthful, Twain reported what he had observed, if perhaps with his own special twist and flair.

What he may have misjudged was the railroad's significance in all this. What carried the editor, the teacher, the missionary, the whisky to the west? The railroad!

The building of the transcontinental line displayed the new industrial north's power at its best and its financially shady side at its worst. Crews driving west featured Civil War veterans, from top to bottom. They had done this before. A witness described it thus:

> On they came. A light car, drawn by a single horse, gallops up to the front with its load of rail. Two men seize the end of a rail and start forward, the rest of the gang taking hold by twos until it is clear of the car. They come forward at a run. At the word of command, the rail is dropped in it place, right side up, with care, while the same process goes on at the other side of the car. Less than thirty seconds to a rail for each gang, and so four rails go down to the minute. Closely behind the first gang come the gaugers, spikers, and bolters, and a lively time they make of it.

The grand "Anvil Chorus" of three strokes per spike, ten spikes per rail, 400 rails per mile went on mile after mile. "Twenty-one million times are those sledges to be swung," the same person noted, "twenty-one million times are they to come down with sharp punctuations, before the great work of modern America is completed."

The construction crews lived in tent cities, "hell on wheels," that fascinated and repelled Americans at the same time. Immorality, violence, and drunkenness marked their path, as they moved West with the rails. With no less vigor, but less sinning, the Central Pacific came east, slowed by the snow-clad, granite Sierra Nevadas. Laborers remained in short supply, so the railroad imported Chinese and on they came. Skeptics doubted the slight Chinese would hold up under the work in the mountains, but they did. The UP coming across the prairie covered more ground than the CP because of its early difficulties getting through the mountains.

Both railroads laid track furiously in 1868-69, planning to gain as much federal money as possible before they met. By the spring of 1869, the two construction crews came in sight of each other, while the surveys paralleled one another. Then, Congressmen suddenly realized that, while intending them to meet, they had enacted no mandatory provision. Nothing prevented them from continuing on to increase subsidies! Congress did. A meeting point at Promontory Summit, Utah was so designated as the place to meet.

Meanwhile, the two companies bet on whose crews were faster. The CP's Chinese won the $10,000 wager, laying ten miles of track in a single day. Monday, May 10, 1869, special trains brought company officials to join those already on hand to link the nation in a railroad wedding. Following a two-minute prayer, officers of the two railroads got down to the serious business of using a silver sledge to drive home a golden spike. To the delight of the construction hardened workers, both missed the first time, but eventually got the job completed. "Done," telegraph lines told the waiting nation. Two locomotives gently moved ahead and touched their cowcatchers, and a bottle of champagne was broken over each. Champagne was the feature of the day according to more than one participant.

The Union Pacific had come 1,038 miles and the Central Pacific, 742 miles. They had spanned the continent in such a rush that months and years would be consumed relocating, regrading, and reconstructing much of their original work. The Union Pacific found itself in all kinds of trouble. Not only was much of it badly built, but financial troubles were a source of unending problems that eventually reached the halls of Congress. The jerry-built line said much about America in those early postwar years.

But, it said much more in a positive manner. Scandals would be forgotten; achievements remained. American enterprise and finances had undertaken and completed a railroad across the continent, from the Missouri River to the Pacific coast in less than five years. Grandiose dreams had been spiked into reality. The West had been opened, its resources stood ready for exploitation. The golden age of railroading was at hand.

Still, not everyone was happy. The railroads could be aggravatingly tardy, painfully slow, and utterly wearisome, as they said, on "one's backside." Mark Twain, not a patient traveler as we have seen, was one of those Americans who was not always enamored by railroad travel. Once, suffering on another dawdling and delayed train, he grew increasingly incensed. When finally the tardy conductor came around, Mark handed him a half fare, customarily the amount that children paid.

Glaring at him, the sarcastic conductor testily inquired, "And are you a child?"

As he often did, Twain proved equal to the occasion.

"No, not any more, but I was when I got on your damn train!"

What a wonderful day, May 10, 1869! The transcontinental railroad spanned the West. Nevertheless, Colorado sat on the sidelines looking forlornly on. What then did the event mean to Coloradans? They had yearned for railroad connections as desperately as anyone in the West. That Colorado needed rail connections was obvious throughout the 1860s, particularly in 1863 and 1864, when the Sioux and Cheyenne cut the overland trails. The "star of empire," as Coloradans liked to call it, had hit a snag.

First Territorial Governor William Gilpin, on his initial night in the territory, told a Denver crowd, from the balcony of the Tremont House, that the transportation difficulties would be overcome. Even better, he predicted on September 10, in his speech to the opening session of the territorial legislature, that the transcontinental railroad would go right through the center of Colorado. That was what his listeners wanted to hear, but within six months he had departed, vanished under financial and political clouds.

Gilpin's replacement, John Evans, proved to be even more of an inveterate railroad promoter. Evans and like-minded Coloradans watched feverishly as the transcontinental railroad bills passed Congress and expected Colorado to be on that line. No one worked harder to gain that needed rail connection than Evans. Still, it did not come to pass. Easier terrain and a lower route through the continental divide lay northward. That was where the Union Pacific went, not over Berthoud Pass, or another equally difficult Colorado pass for a railroad to try to conquer.

When the UP only touched Julesburg in the territory's extreme northeast corner, and then went on to start a rival to Denver in Cheyenne, the decisive moment came to pass. Denver was "too dead to bury," boasted a Cheyenne newspaper. These were dark days indeed. The Kansas Pacific had appeared headed Denver's way, but, with construction funds gone, it bogged down in western Kansas in late 1867. To make matters worse, arch Colorado rival, Golden, might be getting a rail connection, the Colorado Central.

Although no longer governor, Evans, joined by other leading Denver entrepreneurs, now decided to build his own line to tie into the transcontinental route somewhere east of Cheyenne. Financing, as always in Colorado, proved to be the major obstacle. This group could not raise the needed funds, until eastern sources came to the rescue. Both the Kansas Pacific and the Union Pacific were willing to advance some aid, hoping to tap the mining districts. Congress agreed to a land grant. Those additions, combined with funds raised locally, kept the Denver Pacific alive and building. The "hometown" railroad, like most Colorado ventures in these days, was undergirded by outside interests. That proved a high price, eventually.

Finally, in June 1870, Denverites heard the whistle and smelled the smoke; their community was saved. To honor the occasion, Denver celebrated on June 22, although whether a silver spike actually was driven that day to complete construction symbolically appears debatable. It may have been pawned in a saloon on its way down from Georgetown!

Such a small concern aside, Denver's railroad future doubled in size two months later, when the Kansas Pacific arrived. Cheyenne no longer rivaled the "Queen of the Mountain and Plains." Nor did Golden. The Colorado Central built westward into the mountains, northward to Boulder and Fort Collins, and eastward to Denver, though it proved no lasting threat. Financially feeble, and trapped by larger, more aggressive Denver, Golden and its railroad served only as a feeder line.

The Colorado Central did adapt the narrow-gauge track, instead of the standard gauge. By so doing, it saved construction time and costs and found itself with a gauge easily adaptable to mountain railroading. It was the first, but not the last, narrow-gauge Colorado railroad.

The idea for the Colorado Central had come from England and Boston. In the 1870s, the English had become fascinated with narrow gauge, the "railways of the future." Its adherents argued, very plausibly, that it would be much cheaper to build, equip, and maintain than standard gauge. The Colorado Central did not stand alone.

Such arguments convinced a newly-arrived Coloradan, William Jackson Palmer, as well as his English backers. Palmer came to Denver at the time, trying to raise funds for his Denver & Rio Grande, without much success from the cash-strapped locals.

For the Colorado mountains, the three-foot gauge proved ideal. Not only did it have the benefits mentioned, it could handle sharper curves and steeper grades than the standard gauge. A trade off existed, however; narrow gauge engines were less powerful and the cars smaller, thereby hauling less freight and fewer passengers.

Narrow gauge trackage was popular in the United States during the 1870s. By 1880, it reached five percent of the national total, and nearly a third of Colorado's mileage, but, soon after that it started to decline. To simplify operations and cut costs, many railroads shifted to standard gauge during the 1880s. At the least, most added a third outside rail where needed, becoming double gauge, to accommodate equipment from both gauges.

Colorado had its desired railroad connections, as American railroads entered two decades of a building frenzy. When finished, the West was settled. Like an iron arrow, the railroad ran through and divided the lands of the native tribes. The tribes soon became corralled on reservations, as settlers rushed over what once was their homeland. Farmers, cattlemen, and town builders found their promised land, and miners and lumbermen enjoyed an ease of access that only made their natural resources more valuable.

The impact of the railroads proved more than just economic and developmental. One particular change particularly affected Americans. The obvious need for some form of standard time became more crucial after the war, as the railroad spanned the continent. Discussion climaxed with the railroads adopting four time zones on November 18, 1883. The public generally agreed with the idea, although one editor complained that he would rather run his clock on "God's time—not Vanderbilt's!" It would be another thirty-five years before Congress got around to adopting the idea for the nation as a whole.

Coloradans checked their watches and eagerly partook of what was described as a "national barbeque" of selling and giving away the West's natural resources. They relished the chance, finally, to develop their state, which became the "centennial" state in 1876.

Denver became the railroad hub. Out from and into it ran railroads, like spokes from a hub. The Colorado Central continued its drive into the mountains and northward along the foothills. Although it might think of itself as independent of Denver, it was not. Golden never again would challenge its bitter rival. But other railroads did appear. Colorado's number one railroad promoter, John Evans, emerged as the driving force behind the Denver, South Park and Pacific, which ultimately reached Leadville and beyond. He also organized the Denver & New Orleans.

To the south, the Atchison, Topeka and Santa Fe reached Pueblo in 1876. And, in the 1880s, the Chicago, Burlington and Quincy arrived from Illinois and points between. It was touted as the "Cheapest, Best and Quickest" route to Colorado. The Union Pacific eventually arrived in the South Platte Valley, and the Chicago, Rock Island and Pacific tied into Colorado Springs. They all helped to open the eastern plains of Colorado, because, as they advertised, rain followed the rail and plow. For a while, that seemed to be the case. It rained abundantly. Then came the day of reckoning. A dry cycle clamped down on the plains.

The Colorado Midland Railroad entered the fray in 1883. It eventually reached three of Colorado's greatest mining towns—Leadville, Aspen, and Cripple Creek. Colorado mining boomed as never before.

The result of all this was that the plains and mountains had been opened to settlers, tourists, and investors. Railroad was king, even in the "queen city" and throughout its growing hinterlands. Like their rivals elsewhere, all these lines quickly helped end the frontier era and promote development. Generally badly underfinanced, many of Colorado's railroads ran out of steam far short of where they intended to travel. Much to the dismay of cash-short Coloradans, their "home grown" railroad empire quickly came under the control of outsiders, those once-courted, but now thoroughly disliked easterners and Europeans. The Centennial state had become an economic colony. The Union Pacific emerged as the principal villain, swallowing the Denver Pacific, the Denver & New Orleans, the Colorado Central, the Kansas Pacific, and the Denver, South Park & Pacific.

All that aside, the most celebrated and important of all these railroads to Colorado emerged from the fertile mind and driving ambition of William Jackson Palmer. A Civil War veteran, Palmer had been involved in railroading for much of his life, coming west with the Kansas Pacific. He conducted the survey for the railroad into Colorado and came to realize the potential of the southern part of the territory.

The thirty-three-year-old railroader became convinced that a north/south feeder line from Denver, along the mountains into Mexico, would be a perfect match with the transcontinental lines.

However, he arrived in Denver too late in 1869 to tap much beyond enthusiasm and interest, so he looked eastward and across the Atlantic. John Evans, among others, welcomed his idea. "Colorado without railroads, is comparatively worthless," Evans told him. Palmer wholeheartedly agreed.

With the zeal of youth, and the passion of a crusader, Palmer persevered and found the needed funds in England and, to a lesser degree, in the East. Completely devoted to the "cause," his honeymoon took him to England in search of investors. Palmer now was ready to make his dream become reality.

His new Denver and Rio Grande Railway Company would be more than just another railroad company, at least in his mind. Palmer, the businessman, planned to build his own Utopian society. He hoped his company would be "quite a little family," with employees owning stock and partaking in the libraries and bathhouses he planned to "put up for them." He also planned to include schools for their children and lectures for everybody.

The Federal government granted Palmer a 200-foot right-of-way, with twenty-acre spots at ten mile intervals for depots along his projected line. While all this was less than the land grants the UP and CP had received, Palmer accepted it in stride. Not discouraged, the ever-resilient Palmer turned to town building and promotion to move the D&RG along. In 1871, surveyors and track layers set to working. By October 21, rails reached Palmer's new town of Colorado Springs seventy-six miles from Denver. This "colony," based loosely on the highly successful Greeley and Union Colony, proved an amazing success story. Palmer envisioned it as a tourist, health, and cultural community, nestled next to Pike's Peak and "Little London," as it was dubbed, it became all of those. Within a year, Palmer claimed it to be a "thriving city of 1500." So successful did it become, that the D&RG went to work planning other cities along the right-of-way.

Meanwhile, the company also promoted, with its excellent salesmanship, the natural resources. The beauty and healthy climate of the region had succeeded in attracting people to come, which enhancing traffic and trade. Palmer's vision became fact long before it neared his goal of El Paso, Texas.

Then came the national economic crash of 1873, which lengthened into a seemingly unshakable depression. Palmer's dreams crashed momentarily, and the D&RG construction ground to a halt. When the depression lifted in 1877-78, Palmer began again, now challenged by the Santa Fe Railroad for dominance of Colorado and New Mexico. The D&RG had made some enemies along the way by its high-handed methods and financial pressure. Railroads were wonderful for the benefit they brought, but one alone could become a tyrant. Two of them promised competition to the D&RG—and Americans believed in competition. The D&RG was in for a fight, when Leadville exploded on the scene and changed the direction of Palmer's railroad forever.

Both the Santa Fe and D&RG lusted passionately to reach Leadville's silver boudoir, no matter what it took. However, only one easy, short route existed up the narrow Royal Gorge and the

Arkansas River valley. The struggle to reach Leadville nearly destroyed Palmer's dreams. Before it was over, both railroads had fought into the gorge in a "railroad war," had hired gunfighters and lawyers to protect their interests, and eventually it all ended in a costly court fight. As a result, Palmer momentarily lost control of his railroad and finally accepted a compromise.

Palmer gained the Royal Gorge and Leadville, but he lost Raton Pass, Santa Fe, and any hope of ever reaching Mexico. Once he was in the mountains, though, Palmer became excited about other mining districts. None beckoned more alluringly than the transportation-starved and isolated San Juans, far down in southwestern Colorado. Their potentially rich mines provided only part of the lure. Agricultural and coal lands were also there, as was the ever attractive possibility of starting new communities. Before the final settlement of the Royal Gorge entanglement, General Palmer speculated that "Any peace that stops the AT&SF at South Pueblo and gives us Leadville & San Juan, will put the D&RG on stock dividend paying basis."

Located in America's highest and mountainous mining district, the San Juans had been explored and mined since the days of the Spanish coming north out of New Mexico. They had found gold and silver, but the hostility of the Utes and the distance from the Rio Grande Valley meant they were unable to establish permanent settlement or mining operations. They left behind them place names, lost mines, and legends.

Soon after the 1859 Pike's Peak rush, prospectors entered these forbidding mountains. Charles Baker and his party arrived in 1860, promoted the "second California," and singlehandedly created a rush in 1861. On to Baker's Park they came, found little gold, and unhappy Ute neighbors, and left. The onrushing Civil War kept them out, as did the Utes, until the end of the decade. Still, the prospectors and miners persisted. The San Juans were Colorado's "Mother Lode" country. By the mid-1870s, little mining camps, like Silverton, nestled in Baker's Park, allowed mining to continue year round.

These early San Juaners were convinced that their rich mines only awaited the arrival of the best possible transportation to develop into one of America's greatest mining districts. That meant the railroad. With its speed, comfort, all weather potential, and lower rates, it seemed a natural for the San Juans. Seasonal and costly wagon and pack train transportation could not match the iron horse.

Lake City's *Silver World*, September 30, 1876, spoke for many people's hopes when it said, "there will be a railroad in this country within two years, hardly anybody who knows anything about the matter doubts, the question being as to the line and direction." Lake City, Ouray, Animas City, Animas Forks, Sherman—big and small, mining town and mining camp—they all yearned to have railroad connections.

There was no question about Silverton's desires. It <u>had</u> to have a railroad. The *La Plata Miner* (November 29, 1879) left nothing unsaid, "In fact, it is impossible to estimate the great advantage in every way the completion of this road will be to our camp." By that time, the editor and his readers knew that the D&RG was on the way.

This was a "love/love" situation. The San Juaners needed the Denver & Rio Grande, and the railroad saw grand days coming with the completion of their line into this untapped bonanza. However, it was simpler to dream than to build. With the slow recovery from the depression, Palmer, in 1876, started building over La Veta Pass into the San Luis Valley. Even in the midst of the fight with the Santa Fe, he pushed on. By early 1878, the D&RG moved toward Alamosa and, with peace restored and money available, a branch raced on toward Leadville in 1880, Salida being given birth along the way.

Construction had gone fairly easily on the San Juan branch, until the crews moved southward beyond Alamosa. There, as they again turned westward, they encountered the mountains that guarded the San Juan route. Sharp curves, steep grades, and heavy rock work slowed their work. At one point, in order to travel a half-mile distance, the D&RG had to build two-and-a-half miles of track, trestle, and embankment. It cost $140,000 to build one mile of the road! Lured by the idea of "getting rich without working" in the mining regions, the D&RG workers deserted, tired of the daily grind of hard and often dangerous work. The railroad hired others to take their places and hurried on toward its goal. Winter weather hampered work, but finally, on February 1, 1881, the D&RG reached Chama, New Mexico. From there, the route to the newly-started Durango proved relatively easy.

The railroad hurried on, but there was a price to pay— poor construction. This led to numerous derailments and fatal accidents, all of which the D&RG did not care to have publicized. There would still be much work to redo, when the railroad at last reached Silverton. Meanwhile, Palmer and his associates had given birth to the town of Durango. After bickering with Animas City throughout the winter of 1879-80 about terms to make it the railroad hub of southwestern Colorado, the company decided to build its own town. Two miles south down the Animas River, on September 13, 1880, the first survey spike was driven. Just like in Colorado Springs, they organized a real estate company, the Durango Trust, and proceeded to sell lots. The D&RG leadership would also build the smelter across the river, Durango's largest industrial complex for the next generation, and open nearby coal mines. That coal, for fuel and sale, had been a major reason for stopping here. Durango was truly the child of the Denver & Rio Grande.

By Christmas that year, more than 2,000 people crowded into the new "magic city" along the Animas. Animas City became a victim of the D&RG's coming to the San Juans. The train never stopped there. The older community was completely overshadowed by its thriving neighbor, which ultimately swallowed it up.

The first official D&RG train did not arrive until August 1881, amid a two-day celebration. After forcing over-eager Durangoans to remove their hastily constructed buildings from the railroad right-of-way, the railroad hastened on to reach its primary goal, Silverton. Winter and a shortage of rails stopped the D&RG on December 11 at Rockwood, far above the canyon of the Animas River where the tracks had to go. For one short season, that small village basked in the title of "end of tracks." Beyond, however, loomed a mighty problem, how to get down into the canyon and onto Baker's Park.

Where nature had forgotten to carve one, the workers blasted a ledge four hundred feet above the Animas River. Hanging over the edge in jerry-rigged seats, workers drilled holes, placed dynamite, lit the fuse, and then prayed their friends would pull them out of harm's way. The ledge cost a rumored $1,000 a foot to build. Beyond the "high line," as it became known, they constructed a trestle over the river and continued northward. Already behind schedule, the D&RG missed their targeted July 4 arrival in Silverton. Silvertonians held a celebration anyway. Eventually, on, or about, July 13, 1882, the railroad reached Silverton, although the exact date, amazingly, is lost to history.

Silverton's San Juan Herald reported on that day that the final bridge across Mineral Creek was being built. It also correctly forecast, "we will help the railroad, and the railroad will help us. That's about the size of it." The Denver Republican understood even better what had just transpired. The building of the line into the San Juans "is regarded as a marvel in modern engineering and railroad construction." Of course, the paper had ulterior motives for such praise.The line "becomes a highway for Denver."

The idea that had started in England, now had crossed the Atlantic Ocean, climbed the Appalachian Mountains, rolled over the prairies, curled around the Rocky Mountains and had, at last, fought through the Animas River Canyon to reach Baker's Park. The Durango to Silverton Railroad had opened for operation.

CHICAGO & ST LOUIS RR STATION
WESTWARD THE STAR
OF EMPIRE TAKES ITS COURSE
GERMAN COLORADO CO.
ORGANIZED CHICAGO.
AUGUST 24 1869
CARL WULSTE N PRES.
UNDER AUSPICES OF
NATIONAL LAND CO.
C&ST.L.RR
WESTWARD

Courtesy: P. David Smith

Departure of a colony of emigrants for Colorado.

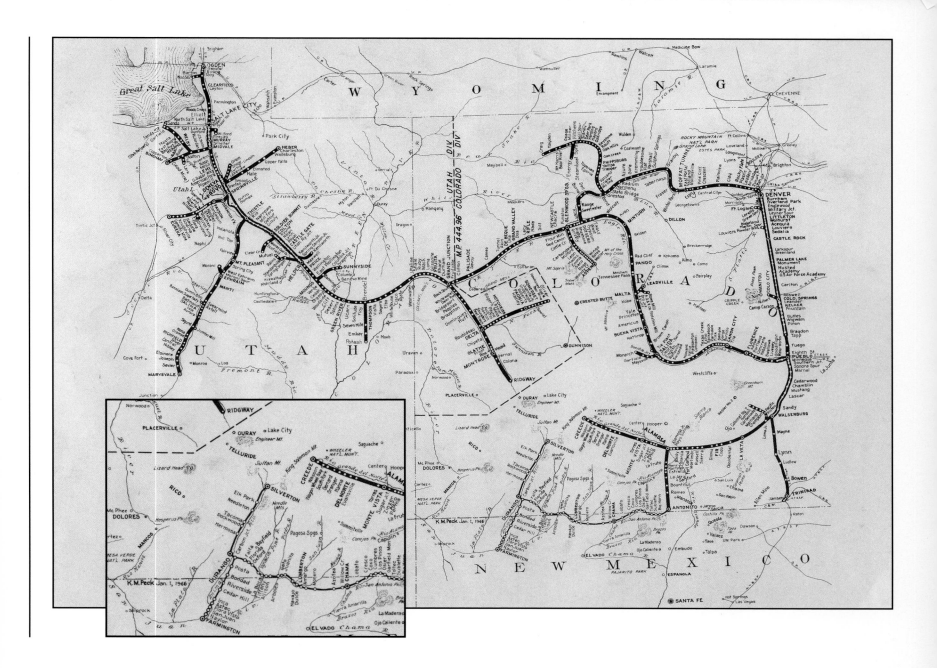

1880s

THE APEX OF TRANSPORTATION

The-long held dream of the San Juan miners and southwestern Coloradans was now crowned with success. The railroad arrived and with it ease of access and year round transportation. For the first time in its history, San Juan County mines topped $1,000,000 in production. Lumbering, coal mining, and agriculture flourished as never before. Meanwhile, La Plata and San Juan Counties' population jumped by a third, and tourists, investors, and traveling salesmen arrived with an ease only imagined before. Even the cost of living went down, but some folks groused about being under the thumb of only one railroad. They already dreamed of a "southern" outlet. That dream would never be fulfilled.

The first decade of the Durango to Silverton line saw the famous western photographer, William Henry Jackson, taking photographs along this spectacular route. Jackson, the official photographer of the Denver & Rio Grande, set the standard for those who would follow. Most of the railroad photographs in this chapter are his.

A photograph and a fishing stop.

The new town of Durango, as it appeared in 1881.

Silverton was a decade old, when this photograph was taken, c1885.

The D&RG needed coal for fuel and sale.   These men helped mine it at Durango's City Coal Mine.

Courtesy: Flora Downtain

Palmer and his railroad wanted to tap the San Juan mining district. These miners at the North Star Mine, and others, eagerly awaited them.

To reach Silverton and the mines took construction of bridges over the Animas in several locations.
The first one was in Durango, the last in Silverton.

The high line, blasted out of this cliff north of Rockwood, cost a thousand dollars a foot to construct.

Courtesy: Durango & Silverton Narrow Gauge Railroad

The high line facinated Jackson, as it has photographers ever since.

Already fishermen were using the railroad to tap those intriguing "holes" in the Animas River.

Tourists and locals on a "columbine" run.

For one brief moment in the winter of 1881-82, Rockwood basked in the fame of being the end of tracks. After that, its fame declined.

1890s

BOOM OR BUST

The 1890s witnessed boom days in San Juan mining, even with the decline in the price of silver and a depression that lasted for nearly six years. Production topped $2,000,000 for the first time in 1895. With the Mears' feeder lines out of Silverton now available to tap nearby districts, the D&RG realized its dream of a decade before. Overall, though, the railroad went through hard times—not the first, nor the last, time.

The Denver to Durango to Ouray, Circle Tour, continued to bring tourists, fewer in number, though. The crash of 1893 and the lingering depression hurt La Plata County and Durango more than it did its neighbor at the other end of the line. By the turn-of-the-century, things were looking up.

The crew stops for a photo in, probably, the Needleton area.

Lumbering prospered with the coming of the railroad.

The Durango smelter, started by D&RG officials, became the region's best.
It was easier to haul ore down track, than to haul supplies and coal up to Silverton.

Generally, the combined passenger and freight train did not stop, despite the view.

Even "ordinary" passenger cars could be spacious.

Denver & Rio Grande cars could be luxurious, especially the private ones.
The original "Alamosa" was wrecked in 1917.

The roundhouse, yards, and depot, as they appeared at the turn-of-the-century.

Tightly packed snow tunnel.

Saguache snowslide, 60 feet deep.

1900-1920

YEARS OF TRANSITION

Turn-of-the-century America! Americans loved it, falling in love with the phonograph, motion pictures, airplanes, electric gadgets, and automobiles. What change! The era of that "bully" of a president, Theodore Roosevelt, that scintillating music rag time (then jazz), the nation wide progressive reform movement, the Titanic, woman's suffrage movement, and the "War to End All Wars" left Americans breathless. It ended with the world-wide holocaust of the 1918-19 flu epidemic.

The Denver & Rio Grande became the Denver & Rio Grande Western, when it tied into its Salt Lake City branch. That was progressive, but not the fact that the railroad was known as "the sick man of Wall Street." It limped along into an age that found competition coming from trucks and cars as highways started to improve and railroads throughout the country faced declining freight and passenger revenue.

Meanwhile, times were also changing on the Durango to Silverton line. Tourism over the "Rainbow Route" decreased, as new attractions and "fads" gained favor. Mining started to collapse, as the 1920s approached, and Durango's boom had ended with the 1890s. Little money had been spent to maintain the line, and wags started to call it "dead and rapidly getting worse!"

Courtesy: La Plata County Historical Society

A particularly bad winter in 1915-16 brought out five engines to buck the snow.

Snow slides were particularly dangerous to railroad operations.
Silverton might be shut off from the world for weeks, and even months, before the tracks were cleared.

Clearing the track was labor intensive in those days.

Tourists will do the darnedest things, when having their photo taken.

Winter storms always caused the railroad problems. Passengers and a herd of horses share a moment.

Times at the depot were not much better than up in the Animas Canyon.

Winter was not the only foe. The "flood of the century" in 1911 took out almost all the bridges on the Animas, as well as surrounding rivers.

When it opened in 1905, the Tacoma Power Plant
was an electric generating marvel. The D&RG ran
special excursion trains for people to see it, and
one of the visitors snapped this photograph.

Courtesy: George Puth Collection   Center of Southwest Studies   Ft. Lewis College

Courtesy: San Juan County Historical Society

Despite declining ore prices and higher costs of deeper mining, a few mines still operated.   The D&RG hauled the ore out of Silverton.

The depot was seldom this crowded, as friends, family, and relatives came to bid goodbye to some boys going off to World War I, the war to make the world "safe for democracy."

Cars take the easy route from Durango to Silverton.

WORST OF TIMES

1920-1940

America went from the "roaring" twenties to the depression thirties—and ended up with a "New Deal." While not all Americans roared, all of them felt the impact of the last two developments in their lives. America would never be the same again.

Two of the segments that did not roar in the 1920s, agriculture and mining, were precisely those that the Rio Grande had long relied on for income. The railroad limped through another twenty years, with competition growing and revenue down. The sick man became sicker. Americans and most Coloradans hardly noticed, because the love affair with the automobile was in full flower. The narrow gauge railroad was becoming the "relic" of an earlier epoch.

Isolated Durango and Silverton noticed this downturn, however. Mining barely hung on during the depression. What once had been the pride and joy of the region, the railroad connections, seemed old-fashioned and costly now. The local highways, meanwhile, were not yet good enough to offset the decline of railroading. In the meantime, lines were being abandoned; by decade's end, only the D&RGW remained in Silverton. The other three short lines were gone. Automobile tourism replaced its railroad counterpart, and the scenic beauty of the Animas Canyon had yet to be rediscovered. The novelty of riding a train remained a future pleasure.

Courtesy: Center of Southwest Studies   Ft. Lewis College

A special train hauled the members of an Elks' Convention.

A freight train on a spring morning.

Locomotive 473 comes in for a "check up."

Silverton yards.

Waiting to be shipped south. During the 1930s, the Shenandoah-Dives was the last major producing mine to ship ore.

Courtesy; Center of Southwest Studies Ft. Lewis College

Sometimes the easiest thing to do is to tunnel through the slide and go on.

Courtesy; Center of Southwest Studies Ft. Lewis College

A 1926 snow slide is tackled by a "ditching machine" in the Needleton area.

Courtesy: Center of Southwest Studies   Ft. Lewis College

Even machines need human help once in a while.

The round house is nearly full while a Rio Grande Southern caboose (the D&RGW owned the line) sits in the yard.

The railroad yards look quiet, as a locomotive leaves with a full tender load of coal.

1940-1960

HOLLYWOOD & TOURISM TAKE OVER

World War II brought America out of the depression and into a new era. Then Americans loved "Ike" and his "modern Republicanism" in the 1950s as the tensions of the Cold War added yet another contemporary dimension to the changing times. Television made its debut and America would never be the same again. Meanwhile, airplanes and automobiles took over a larger share of the country's transportation.

For the Denver & Rio Grande Western these were challenging times, challenging in just trying to stay alive. One after another, the company abandoned more nonprofitable lines and concentrated efforts on keeping the main line in business. Before these decades became history, the Rio Grande Southern was gone leaving only the tracks into Durango and Silverton remaining. Narrow gauge trains and lines were an anachronisms in this modern age.

For the Silverton run, these too were challenging, and also fascinating, decades. Freight and passenger travel declined alarmingly with the completion of paved Highway 550 from Durango to Ouray. Then Hollywood discovered the beauty of the San Juans and the spectacular line through the Animas Canyon. A new era dawned. By the late fifties, however, talk surfaced of abandoning the line, but Durango and Silverton folk would not let that happen. Finally, thanks to the movies and determined local promotion, tourists started to travel the narrow gauge into "yesteryear."

Courtesy; Center of Southwest Studies Ft. Lewis College

Filling the sand dome for another run.

A double-header prepares to leave Durango.

A quiet 1950s day at the depot, with the smelter active across the river processing uranium ore.

One of the increasingly rare passenger and freight trains on its way to Silverton.

Rocky Mountain rail fans rode this special to savor the sights and thrills of "old time" railroading.

Meanwhile, 463 continued to bring passengers and a little freight to Silverton.

"Denver & Rio Grande" in 1952 featured this collision between engines 519 and 268.

A classic photograph of snow plowing.

The last run of a strictly passenger train occurred in 1950.

Courtesy: Denney Schilthuis Collection   Center of Southwest Studies   Ft. Lewis College

Round house and yard, as they appeared in 1955.

Hollywood arrives! "A Ticket to Tomahawk" (1950) featured the antler-bedecked "Emma Sweeny."

Butch & Sundance leave the robbery.

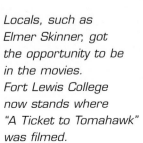

Locals, such as Elmer Skinner, got the opportunity to be in the movies. Fort Lewis College now stands where "A Ticket to Tomahawk" was filmed.

The film extravaganza, "Around the World in Eighty Days" (1956) was partly filmed on the Durango to Silverton line.

Jimmy Stewart and Brandon DeWilde were two of the stars of the 1957 western, "Night Passage."

The unplanned destruction of the express car, a miscalculation by the film company. Only the safe was supposed to be "dynamited."

Courtesy: Walter Conrad.

Courtesy: San Juan County Historical Society

The end of the Hollywood era came with the filming of "Butch Cassidy and the Sundance Kid" in 1969. This scene was shot south of Durango, as the gang moves in to rob the express car.

1960s

A FULL-TIME TOURIST ATTRACTION

During the 1960s, the Durango to Silverton line became, for all practical purposes, a tourist attraction. The D&RGW might claim it was not in the entertainment business, but this segment of its system survived because of tourism and the growing love affair of Americans with their western frontier heritage. The Animas Canyon and its narrow gauge line were one of the most intriguing remnants of that era. Railroad management finally conceded and developed the site around the depot as "Rio Grande Land."

By the late 1960s, the little line was completely isolated, as the tracks from Alamosa to Durango were abandoned. Eventually, the Antonito-to-Chama segment of that line would also be turned into a tourist attraction. Now, the Durango and Silverton would have to survive by tourism alone.

Courtesy: Robert Trennert

Daily Silverton train, 1963.

The roundhouse crew "cleans fire" of 473, prior to its Silverton run.

Engine 476 on its way to pick up its passenger cars.

Roundhouse and turntable on a fall day in September 1960.

A journey into "yesteryear."

A train load of happy and tired tourists pass the Hermosa tank on their way back to Durango, ahead of a storm.

Number 497 is about to depart for Alamosa in July 1967.
Locomotive 473 is headed for Silverton in a sequence of departures that will soon end.

The dawn of a September 1966 morning. Number 476 gets ready to haul tourists to Silverton.

Courtesy: Robert Trennert

A train awaits its passengers in Silverton.

Coaling for another run.

1970s

COMING OF AGE

The decade of the seventies saw the Denver & Rio Grande's Silverton branch suffer a devastating setback with the flood of 1970 and the destruction of about six miles of track. Without missing a beat, it rebuilt the line, much to the relief of Durango and Silverton folk.

The railroad, now completely isolated, had become a major tourist attraction and an essential economic pillar for both communities. With the gradual improvement of the district around the Durango depot and increased trains with a longer season, the scenic line rightfully secured a place as a star in the national railroad attractions and was gaining an increasing following from elsewhere.

Despite this, the D&RGW remained adamant about not being in the entertainment business. By decade's end, they were seriously looking for a buyer for the line. That left the two towns and the region wondering what the future might bring.

Courtesy: Richard Gilbert

The high line thrilled passengers, as it had for the past ninety years.

The roadbed and tracks were not a pretty sight in September 1970.

A passenger train enters the high line, obviously an area not bothered by the 1970s flood!

Passengers hardly realized what flood damage had been done to the roadbed and tracks by mid-decade.

Courtesy: Center of Southwest Studies   Ft. Lewis College

The dark days of fall were followed by the joyful days of spring, with the trains back in Silverton.

Crossing Hermosa Creek with the mountains just around the curve.

Trains and locomotives fascinate visitors who did not remember the "glory days" of railroading only a couple of generations ago.

Number 476 departs for Silverton.

Checking 473 at the round table.

Courtesy: Richard Gilbert

Durango has changed mightily since 1881, but the depot and roundhouse would have looked familiar to old-timers.

1980s

GOODBYE, DENVER & RIO GRANDE

Finally, the long awaited sale of the railroad came about. For the moment, time froze as locals wondered what might happen. The new owner, Charles Bradshaw, Jr. purchased the renamed Durango & Silverton Narrow Gauge Railroad in March 1981. After more than one hundred years, the Denver & Rio Grande retired from the narrow gauge railroad business.

New ownership produced new vigor. New equipment, greater advertising, and improved community relations at both ends of the line promised a brighter tomorrow. It worked. Ridership went up.

Then, in February 1989, the railroad suffered another major setback, when the roundhouse burned. Yet despite damage to six locomotives, the trains were running that spring. Within a year, a larger and a more modern roundhouse was built, utilizing what walls were left of the older structure.

Courtesy: Amos Cordova

Locomotive 482 arrives to once again be part of an operating narrow gauge railroad.

In the canyon, with Silverton coming up.

Winter trains to the Cascade Wye were a popular new feature.

Night in the railroad yards.

Passengers still ride in style in the Alamosa Parlor Car.

The "Pop" car follows the trains to help prevent spark-started fires and retrieve items that may have fallen from the cars.

The morning after the disastrous roundhouse fire.

Charles Bradshaw, Jr. dedicates the new roundhouse.

It almost looks like a mixed train of yesteryear, but passengers were its main "cargo."

Silverton, unlike its neighbor to the south, has not changed all that much in the twentieth century.

New roundhouse and old depot, plus a host of cars and equipment, are ready for a new season.

1990s

STEAMING TOWARDS A NEW MILLENNIUM

The Durango & Silverton chugs steadily into its second century in the 1990s. Under the leadership of Charles Bradshaw, Jr., the railroad continued the progress noted in the previous decade. A general tourism downswing in the four corners region was reflected in a passenger ridership decline that righted itself as those ten years ended.

In 1997, Bradshaw sold the line to First American Railways, a company that ran a Florida "fun" train as well. The combination did not work successfully and, within slightly over a year, businessman and real estate developer Allan Harper purchased the Durango & Silverton. With enthusiasm, a fine sense of history, and a dedication to preserving the railroad's heritage, he and his staff guided it toward the new millennium.

The railroad continues its nearly 120 year-old-legacy of transporting folks from Durango to Silverton, across the spectacular miles that still fascinate and amaze travelers. As our friend, Mark Twain, wrote about travel, "broad, wholesome, charitable views of men and things cannot be acquired by vegetating in one little corner of the earth all one's lifetime."

The photographs that follow offer a collage of images of the Durango & Silverton, as it steams on into history and the future at the same time, while providing enjoyment in the present. They were photographed by Glen Crandall in 1998-99.

EPILOGUE

If the statement Shakespeare wrote, "what's past is prologue," needs to be proven, the Durango & Silverton provides a rousing answer. The railroad originally created Durango and brought Silverton and its mining district into a bonanza era. It supplied the means to bring supplies, investors, settlers, and tourists, and to ship local products. Thus, the D&RG further developed and strengthened the economy of an isolated part of Colorado and the entire four corners region.

The Denver & Rio Grande promoted and advertised the region. The D&RG underwrote expansion of other railroad lines, and was involved in a variety of local and regional issues from smelters, politics, and coal mining to town building. It also negatively affected communities it bypassed and even its neighbors did not always love their "savior." In that collision, it reflected railroad contemporaries throughout the United States.

The narrow gauge line is still here and the trains travel to Silverton and back, which is more than may be said for most of its colleagues. Undaunted, it continues to advertise, promote, stimulate the local economy, bring in tourists by the hundreds of thousands and save a Victorian heritage. In the end, the Durango & Silverton has preserved the sights, smells, mountain excursion, and atmosphere of a vanished America. What more could its founders and railroad men of the past century plus ask. May the same be said, a century from now!

Courtesy: Robert Royem Durango & Silverton Narrow Gauge Railroad

The Galloping Goose never galloped on the Silverton branch until 1998.
Its home had been the Rio Grande Southern.

The train heads for Silverton, on a spring 1999 morning, just as it has for the past one hundred seventeen years.

The past is still here in 1998. An 1875 wood burning Baldwin 4-4-0 locomotive enjoys a day on the Durango & Silverton. It originally hauled passengers and ore from Eureka, Nevada.